PIECE-A-WAY CROSSROADS

PIECE-A-WAY CROSSROADS

Gloria Gipson Suggs

CONTENTS

Acknowledgement

The author wishes to thank her immediate family, Franklin, Michael, Linda, and Langston for the love, patience, suggestions, and encouragement given during the writing of Piece-A-Way Crossroads.

She would also like to thank her parents, sisters, brothers, and the many relatives, friends, and families of North Mississippi who helped to shape the way she viewed life in rural America.

Introduction

Piece-A-Way Crossroads is a story of fiction that is based on the life of a couple, Peter and Rhea, who lived in Marshall County, Mississippi during the 1930s through the 1960s. One of their daughters, Jeannie, invites the readers to come piece-a-way with her as she tells their story. She invites them to come along and meet some of the people and see some of the places her parents encountered during difficult, turbulent and sometimes beautiful times; The Great Depression and the desegregation issues. To show how her parents, Peter and Rhea, dealt with these difficult and sensitive situations and issues, Jeannie integrates stories, poetry, and art in a story telling format.

COME PIECE- A- WAY WITH ME

Come piece- a- way with me
I am afraid
I have not traveled this path before
I have not gone that distant path
That leads to a distant shore

Come, hold my hand
Show me the way
Help me prepare myself for things ahead
Help me gather my thoughts
Tell me what to say

Come piece- a- way with me
Down the long road
And into the dark
I am just a little afraid
I hope my nerves want soon depart

For generations, you came with me
Down the road
A few miles from home
The distant crossroads I had to travel
I knew I would not be alone

      GLORIA GIPSON SUGGS

Ancestral History: The People Who Made the Difference

Leah:
A Long Ways From Home

Leah was brought from Africa to Mobile, Alabama, in the early 1840s. She was sold and transported to the McGhee Plantation in Florence, Alabama. While in slavery, she had a son named Jeremiah. She died in Florence during the 1860s

Jeremiah and Ruth:
Freedom and Land In Marshall County

When Leah's son, Jeremiah, was set free from slavery, he met and married a lady named Ruth who was a descendant of the Native American tribe, Choctaw. They had 10 children, one of whom was named Sarah. They thought about joining the Underground Railroad in search of a better life after slavery until they heard land could be bought for $0.25 an acre in Marshall County. So Jeremiah, Ruth, and their family, left Florence, Alabama and traveled on foot to a plantation called, Twenty-Four. This plantation was located on the Benton and Marshall County lines, near old highway 7. In order to earn and save money, they worked as sharecroppers on this plantation for several years. Then, Jeremiah moved his family to Marshall County in 1906 and bought land that was part of the Graves Plantation.

FORTY ACRES AND A MULE

When they got their papers
Stating they were free
Generations of bonded brothers
Shouted out with glee
Some felt it did not matter
As long as they were free
They were given a mule and forty acres
And forty dollars to buy some seeds

North they went looking for fortune
East and west- for fame
South they went seeking shelter
And to see a familiar face
They were bonded together as brothers
For generations or two
They united again as brothers
Forty acres and a mule didn't do

They united again as brothers
Forty acres and a mule didn't do

Jeremiah and Ruth lived in a log house called a dog trot that was used by hunters during the plantation era. Their adult children lived in clap board row houses that was located across the road and down from their house. The log house was opened in the center that had a cistern in the planked-in breezeway and 2 rooms to the right side of the hallway and three room on the left side. It had a kitchen on the back left side of the house that had a large cast iron stove that was used for cooking. The other rooms contained small fireplaces or wood burning heaters.

     GLORIA GIPSON SUGGS

When Ruth died, her wake and funeral was held at this house in their bedroom which doubled as parlor. This room was located on the front right side of the house. Ruth was buried in the cemetery of Hudsonville CME Church. Jeremiah died in the late 1940s. His funeral and burial was held at this same church. It is believed he was a hundred years old when he died.

Isaac:
The Community Merchant

Their son Isaac continued to live in this house after Jeremiah died. He suffered from a seizure disorder and never married. He was able to support himself by raising cotton and corn on the 20 acres he inherited from his parents. Isaac owned a mule which he named "Hemp". Hemp was a good work mule that had a good sense of time. At 12 o'clock sharp, Hemp would neigh and stop pulling the plow because he could tell instinctively or by the position of the sun, that it was time for lunch. At that same time, someone at a different location would ring the dinner bell, verifying to the children his mule's accuracy of telling time.

Isaac planted, cultivated, gathered, and sold his own crops. Only if he were running late he would ask for help. He knew how to read and write well enough to take care of all of his business matters.

He sold goods out of a green doomed-top trunk to people in the community. If you went to his house, you could buy the same products you could purchase at the country store, including coal oil. He sold goods such as chewing and bubble gum, candy snuff, cigars, and cigarettes out of a trunk. Loose-leaf paper, tablets, pencils, pens, and crayon were also sold. Isaac kept kerosene on hand for lamp fuel and fixing hair. Seasoning for food and thread for sewing were also available.

Isaac's trunk was well organized at all times by color and type of goods. The smell of his trunk was so inviting to us we were always tempted to buy something every time he opened it. The trunk looked like a pirate's treasure chest; dark green in color, domed top with a raised design on the outside, and a painted picture of a fancy lady inside.

Isaac would sell candy and chewing gum out of his pockets at gatherings and church activities.

When church services were long and stomachs were empty, we always knew that Isaac would be outside with plenty of cures for what ailed you. When he was not at home with his trunk, he would advertise his wares in his hand, displaying red, green, and yellow wrappers of gum and candy. We knew the prices and we knew he had the goods, so selection and exchange of money was all that was necessary.

When his health started to fail, he moved in the house with Sarah, his sister, and her husband Jacob. When Jeremiah's house became vacant, children use to hold hands when passing his house for fear of hearing sounds and seeing lights in the parlor room window where his wife Ruth died. Isaac died in Sarah and Jacobs' house in the early 1960s. His funeral and burial was held at the same church of the resting place of his parents.

Isaac was also a photographer. Today the community is grateful to him for preserving past generations in pictures.

Jacob and Sarah: Community Planners With A Big Red Truck

Jacob was the husband of Sarah, who was the daughter of Jeremiah and Ruth. Jacob, a decent of the Cherokee Tribe and Africans, was the son of Moses who moved to Marshall County from Grand Junction, Tennessee. They belonged to Gatewood Church. They were leaders of social, economic, religious, and educational activities in the community. Their home was a gathering place for major and minor family and community events. They were the owners of the big red truck. Everyone between Mount Pleasant, Slayden, Holly Springs, and Byhalia, knew them or had heard of them.

　　　　GLORIA GIPSON SUGGS

Big Red Truck

Big red truck, you came by here
We were all dressed up in shopping gear
We limbed your ladder, big and small
Grandma, grandpa, families, and all
Your big wooden bed looked so tall
We had to hang on for fear we'd fall

Big red truck, you moved so fast
Through childhood and adulthood, we say you pass
Pass the highways and byways on the way to town
You always had room for all around
From dusk to dawn you brought them all
Home, town, and back again- you never missed a call

Their farm had a large fishing pond which produced such large fish it became a community gathering ground for adults and a swimming place for children.

Jacob built his house with the help of his neighbors and sons. This favor was then returned when they needed a home. It was a plank board house with 2 room on both sides of a hallway and a kitchen on the back. It had a large dining room in the center of the house. Sarah use to enjoy serving breakfast to their grandchildren in this room. They would come and spend the night at their house from time to time. The dining room contained a large potbellied stove that doubled as a heater. Sarah would serve them home made preserves, freshly cut beacon, buttered biscuits, and hot coco or milk.

Large planked porches flanked the front and back of the house. The porch on the back wrapped around a potbellied cistern.

He also built a large barn, stables, smoke houses, chicken coops, and a tool shed on his place.

There was also an old log cabin he use to rent out to different people from time to time. A lady named Martha was the last person to stay in this house. Children loved to visit her during the Christmas season. She was a warm-hearted person that had a cuckoo clock with a bird that would always put on a good show.

Jacob and Sarah's home served as a meeting place every Wednesday, for their children, grandchildren, and other members of the community who wanted to attend. They stressed the importance of investing in land, believing in God, and getting an education. They emphasized that these things were building blocks on which to construct sound foundations for future generations. Their teaching paid off many times over.

Their ancestors live throughout the United States and several foreign countries. Their occupations vary from farmers, teachers, businessmen, doctors, lawyers, musicians, and politicians to administrators and homemakers. Jacob and Sarah's legacy became:

"Always stress family unity, work hard, save money, and invest in real estate. Once you succeed, reach back and help those that need it through encouragement or finance."

Martin and Rachael:
The Molasses Man And The Midwife

artin's parents were Richard and Jewel. They were born
in Moscow, Tennessee. Rachael's parents were Albert and
Katherine. Katherine was born in Richmond, Virginia in the early
1850s and Albert was born in Montgomery, Alabama. In the late
1840s. They all were descendants of African and the native tribe,
Choctaw. Martin and Rachael lived west of Slayden. They were
members Isom Chapel C. M. E. Church. They were the parents of
Rhea who married Peter. They had 9 other children. Their home was
a log cabin which Martin helped to build. This house was constructed
with 2 rooms, a hallway, and porch facing west on the front of the

     GLORIA GIPSON SUGGS

house. The kitchen, dining room, and another porch was built onto the back facing west.

Although their beginnings were humble, love and hard work were their key ingredients to their success. They knew what it was like to be poor, so after their marriage they literally walked out of sharecropping into becoming successful landowners. With a basic knowledge of quilting sewing, weaving, and farming, this couple became known at local fairs for their skills in crafts and artwork, which they also taught their children. They sold goods at county fairs and throughout the community as another method of making money besides selling farm produce and livestock. Coming from Seminole and African background, they believed that the gifts or talents given them should be used as a profession, because then they would enjoy doing the job and do their best at it.

Rachael was also a midwife and delivered most of her grandchildren and many other children in the community and beyond. If Rachael ran into problems during a delivery, someone would go to Mt. Pleasant and ask Dr. Brown to rush out to help.

Martin was a farmer who also made molasses for people in surrounding communities in the fall. People would get the molasses mill set up for him 2-3 weeks in advance of him coming to an area. Sleeping and eating provisions would be made for him with the family that lived closest to the mill. Someone would also be assigned to bring his lunch to the mill at 12 o'clock sharp. If the family that he made molasses for could not pay for his services, he would accept so many cans of molasses in return.

After Martin died in the early 1960s, Rachael continued to live in their home. One day, Rhea and one of her daughters, Jeannie, came to visit. They stayed until late evening and decided it was too late to walk home through the dense woods. So, Rachael made plans for them to stay the night. Rachael's bedroom was on the left side of the hallway which had a rocking chair with a large Bible laying on its seat. The room that Rhea and Jeannie slept in was on the right side of the hallway.

At 12 o'clock, Rhea and Jeannie were awaken by a rattling sound coming from the hallway. Rhea got up and lit the kerosene lamp that was on the mantle over the fireplace and rushed into the hallway. Jeannie immediately followed her. To their amaze, the high back rocking chair was rocking back and forth. The large Bible, which was closed when they went to bed, was now opened. The pages were making rattling sounds as they sled together and folded down at its upper left hand corner. Rhea and Jeannie watched this unbelievable sight for about a minute or two and rushed into Rachael's room and awakened her. Rachael rushed quickly with them back into the hallway. She did not seem concerned about what she say taking place. She said, "This happens every night at midnight. The Bible opens up to a different page and the page folds down and points to a different verse." Rhea and Jeannie went closer to the Bible to see what verse was pointed at this time. It was John 4:14 which read;

"And we have seen and do testify that the Father sent the Son to be the Savior of the world."

Rhea asked Rachael, "What do you think this all means?" Rachael replied, "Well, I think this is Martin's way of letting me know that he is in Heaven with the Lord". At 1 o'clock, the rocking

     GLORIA GIPSON SUGGS

chair stopped rocking and the Bible closed. For Rhea and Jeannie, that was a blessed and unforgettable night.

After Rachael died 20 years later, it is said that this Bible was given to someone who worked at one of the colleges in Memphis. It was not heard from after that time.

Rachael always loved flowers. She would plant flowers all around the house and they would put on a good show during reunion time.

Grandma's Flower Garden Still Looks Good

Sunflowers act as backdrop
Daisies fill in the middle
Petunias serve as border plants
For easy watering with a kettle

Zinnias stand in-between
The red Irises and blue Tulips
Pink Crepe Myrtle near the house
Serve as shade for the ferns

Primroses on the picket fence
Yellow Cactus in a tub
Some Four O'clock just sprouted out
Behind the chimney next to the wood

Some Marigolds are in full bloom
Purple Tulips just opened up
A trench around a Formosa tree
Contains budding Buttercups

The Morning Glories look real good
Beneath that red Hibiscus
The Magnolia tree is in full bloom
On the porch sat a bucket of white Carnations

Those Mother-in-Law Tongues are holding their own
So are the Bird-in-the-Nest
The Sweet Williams came up again
The yellow Mums will be next

That Dogwood tree in the corner
Still supports those Honeysuckles vines
That Mulberry tree still is home for the bees
And the Cedar trees are doing just fine
Grandma's flower garden still looks good

Rachael was short and pleasingly plump. Martin was tall and lean. People still remember the stories told of how they met, fell in love, married, and raised their children. They also told how they loved to dance together because of the attention given them due to their contrast in size and height. They were known for overcoming major obstacles by using their inborn talents to turn dim situations into success stories.

BARBARA:
THE STORK LADY

Barbara was a midwife that lived in the community. She delivered at least 2 generations of children from the early 1940s to the late 1950s. Children use to look for the stork because we knew each time Barbara showed up a baby would soon follow.

Barbara travels to her destination by walking or riding horseback in her younger days and by wagon and car in the later 1950s.

She would usually come 2 or 3 days before delivery time to observe the expecting mother, so if complications developed, she would instruct the family to rush and get Dr. Miller from Holly Springs for the task. During this "stay", which was usually a 3 days period, the best was prepared for Barbara in the form of food and living accommodations. After the delivery, if no money was available, eggs, meat, or other produce, was given to her for services rendered.

Besides being a midwife, Barbara was noticed because of her appearance and voice. She sported a thick mustache. She could sing well, too. She was given the job of being a song leader at Hudsonville Church, especially during devotional and revival services. Her voice was so deep that it seemed to shake the entire church. Her delivery was so powerful that emotions moved through the congregation in the form of shouts, laughter, and tears. She had her own style of singing, which came to be known throughout the community. Her sound is still alive today, thanks to such a pleasant impression made by Barbara, the beautiful lady with the mustache.

A Place Called Home

PETER AND RHEA:
THEY SAID IT WOULD NOT LAST

Peter and Rhea eloped and married during the mid-1920s. Peter was eighteen and so was Rhea. They eloped and were married at dawn the next day by Rev. Shaw. It was several days before Rhea's parents, Martin and Rachael, found out where their oldest daughter was and what had happened.

SOUTHEAST COUNTY LINE

We'll meet there right at midnight
Or just about a quarter to nine
What will they say?
About us meeting this way
At that southeast county line

The moon beams will act as guide posts
Or treasures for lovers to find
Will they miss us when
Dusk comes again
At that southeast county line

Look for me in the shadows
Between the grove of slender pines
We will run away
And marry by day
At that southeast county line

This couple's first home was located just north of Peter's parents' house, Sarah and Jacob, where 6 of their children were born. This house was a white wooden frame house with a tin top. It had 2 fireplaces, and 2 bed rooms that doubled as sitting rooms, a hallway, and a kitchen. This house had no porches even though they were extremely important back then. They were an extension of the house and if you needed more room, you could get one of the local carpenters to close them in.

THEIR SECOND HOME

In the mid 1930s, Rhea and Peter bought a place that had an old Louisiana Tutor house on it. Eleven of their seventeen children were born Eleven of their seventeen children were born there and 2 died, Leah and Jeremiah. They were members of Gatewood MB Church which was located several miles east of their home.

Like some plantations, this family's home site reflected the lifestyle of the post slavery days. The original farm site consisted of six hundred and forty acres of land and was part of the Graves Plantation. This property housed a main house, cook house barn, cribs, stables, cotton gin, and chicken coops. A major road that went past this house accommodated shipment of supplies and produce throughout the township and surrounding communities. Later, the cotton gin was moved to another community, north of Rhea and Peter's home called Slayden. All families who settled in this area raised cotton, corn, cattle, chickens and livestock as the former owners did.

Peter and Rhea bought the house and one-fourth of the land around it. It was a two-story house that had 4 large columned porches, 6 fireplaces (2 upstairs and 4 downstairs), and a large entrance hall with 2 doors that opened onto the front and back porches.

It had 2 staircases. One staircase lead from the entrance hall to an area which consisted of a balcony and an inner room which was called the girl's room. The other closed-in stairwell was off the main downstairs bedroom, adjacent to the dining room. It lead up to the boy's room. A door leading from the boy's room opened into an area over the dining room. This area was supposed to have been a library.

The house served as a center for large social gatherings, which extended onto the large flowered and wooded yard.

Gutters were attached to overhangs to supply rainwater to the cistern, a storage in the grown that kept water cool and fresh. A bucket tied on the end of a rope was used to pull the water up when needed. The Cistern was constructed of bricks that were laid in a well dug from 10-20 ft. deep. The external portion was belly shaped, about 2ft. above the ground, and had a cement lid that attached to the gutter through an opening.

The large fireplaces, which were 5ft. wide and 4ft. high, served as cooking and heating furnaces in early years. They also made a convenient and safe entry for Santa Claus on Christmas Eve.

The dining room also served as a study, canning, and quilting room. Peter made an 8x4 foot table with 4 round legs and rollers that he cut from the railroad tiles Peter worked as a crewman for the road department when the highways in this area were being paved. Repairs on the railroad were also taking place at that time near a surround town. Workers on the road and railroad were allowed to take away unused or discarded material, so he was able to take what he needed to build the table. Rhea bought table clothes from Golden Rules in Holly Springs. If she could not find the right size, she would

     GLORIA GIPSON SUGGS

make one by sewing flour sacks together. The dining room had a large window that let in plenty of light in the daytime. It had a large fireplace and mantle that held oil lamps for night light. The dining room table was rolled aside to make room for quilting racks when Rhea hosted quilting parties.

The Quilting Lamp

Sell me a good lamp to quilt by
I have pieced a four, eight, and sixteen patch
And started a Texas and a broken star
All the ladies will gather
At my house supper
It will be very dark

Sell me a good lamp to quilt by
Let it match my Sunday china
Or pick up the flowers on the wall
The glow must be bright
So our stitches will be right
The shade should be tapered and tall

The large kitchen was adjacent to the dining room and contained a large fireplace that shared a chimney with the fireplace in the dining room. This fireplace was used for cooking along with a stove that was vented into its chimney as a primary cooking source. Peter kept his harmonica on the mantle shelf in this room where he taught his sons Peter Jr., Stetson, and Elson how to play. The kitchen originally had 1 window and 2 doors, one opened onto a porch on the west side of the house and the other opened onto a porch on the east side. The east side door was later changed into a window after the east side porch was torn down. This door was used as a service door from the cook's house that was located on the east yard of this house during the plantation days. The kitchen had a large storage closet that was back to back to the one in the dining room.

The large living room or parlor was located on the west side of the entrance hall. It had 2 windows facing the north, one facing the west, and one facing the south. It housed a closet that was adjacent to a large fireplace that was decorated with a fancy mantel piece.

Logan, a local electrician who lived on Slayden Road, wired this house for electricity in the early 1950s and placed simple light fixtures in the center of every room. The fixture in the dining room looked like a fancy chandelier to me because of the reflection of light on the bulb from the tall eastern window. We also used the dining room as a meeting and prayer room on Thursdays. This gave each family member who was present a chance to refocus goals, voice concerns, make suggestions, and bind closer to the family in a spiritual manner.

The fireplace in the dining room used the same chimney as the fireplace in the kitchen. The chimney went through the second-story level that was supposed to have been made into a library when the house was built. The fireplace opening over the dining room upstairs was never complete but covered over as part of the floor. Sometimes sounds could be heard coming from this opening.

Just Another Ghost Story?

As children we heard that this house may have served as a place of refuge for wounded and dying soldiers after the Civil War. For many years, ghost tales were told describing "faces" that were seen and "cries" that were heard from these refugees. The sounds from this chimney added validity to the tales.

Rhea and Peter's son, JC, gave a detailed account about seeing a ghost in the form of twenty white horses pulling a chariot. He was outside when he saw this gghost sighting up the hill, just north of the house. He said it was moving east to west in front of the lot and garden area, so this house may have been haunted, after all.

Their son, Boone, said he saw some long bent fingernails, and even though the man was sitting on the front, Boone clearly described that the ghost was tall, gray-haired and narrow bearded. The man was dressed in a long robe that had colorful stripes and designs resembling that of a Native American Tribe. It was an unforgettable and frightening sight to behold, according to Boone. The dogs must have seen it to, as it took about an hour for them to settle down and stop barking after the ghost disappeared.

Education is the Key

Peter and Rhea went to one-room schools. They only completed the 5th grade, but learned quickly in the "school of life", after their marriage and children, how to run and manage a farm. Peter was successful at farming because he learned how to respect the environment in order to make the best yield from principle crops of cotton and corn. He attended workshops at the experimental farm on crop rotation and soil conservation methods. He learned about animal husbandry to produce high grade meat from hogs, cattle, and chicken. He also enlisted in the Navy for a while in order to help support eleven children which they had by the early 1940's.

Rhea was a skillful homemaker who attended home demonstration workshops to learn about new utensils and techniques in processing foods at the experimental farm. She shared her knowledge by holding canning parties and teaching others in the community what she learned. She was a self-taught master at quilting, embroidering, and crocheting. She also made most of her family's clothes, where she drew her patterns on brown paper from looking at pictures in catalogs.

Peter and Rhea knew the importance of education and made the opportunity available to each of their surviving fifteen children. Two of their children died as infants. Each of their children accepted this challenge in a different way and at a different rate. They stressed the importance of being an individual and did not compare on child's progress with another. This progressive concept in child development at that time made them pioneers, because some members of the community were placing emphasis on survival, not education. Their children attended Henry Elementary one and two-room school. They attended high school at Rust, MI, Sand Flat, and St. Mary's.

Twelve of their children went on to receive associate, bachelor, and master degrees. Sarah Rachael received a BA degree in English and Frenchie received BA degrees in English and History from Rust College. Mark earned a BS degree in Science Education from Rust College. Natalie received her BS degrees in Biology and Sociology and Jeannie received BS degrees in Biology and Chemistry from Rust College. Benjamin received a BS degree in Science Education and Harvester received a BS degrees in Mathematics from Mississippi Industrial College (MI). Laura earned her BS degrees in Biology and Chemistry from Lemoyne Owens College in Memphis, Tennessee. Eva received a BS degree in Nursing from the University of Memphis (U of M), Memphis, Tennessee. Reva received a BA degree in Management from Upper Iowa State University in Des Moines, Iowa. Elson earned a BA degree in Tools and Die from Northwest Mississippi Junior College in Senatobia, Mississippi. Boone earned an AA degrees in Social Science and Criminal Justice from Tennessee State University in Nashville, Tennessee.

Later on, Jeannie received a M.Ed. degree in Curriculum Development and Instruction from Memphis State University (U of M), Memphis, Tennessee. Harvester received a MA degree in Administration and Supervision degree from the University of Mississippi (Ole Miss) in Oxford, Mississippi.

If Peter and Rhea could have bestowed degrees, they would have given the following degrees of life to their 3 children who did not receive them. Peter Jr., a DL degree in love of life, adventure and for his dedication and work on the farm; JC, a DL degree for his artwork, patience and caring nature towards people, especially to his parents; and to Stetson, a DL degree for his great sense of humor and his role in the civil rights movement.

Peter and Rhea were married to each other for more than 60 years. They credited their success in marriage to being able to accept people as they are and not for what you want them to be. Their legacy was "Get a good education and stand up for your civil rights"

 GLORIA GIPSON SUGGS

MEMORIES, WIND-BLOWN

Memories, wind-blown
Stripped of shutters, tin and paint
Tilting to the left
As I lose my upward reach
But oh, how I remember
Those days of yesteryear
When I was in my glory
And a major road passed by hear

Memories, wind-blown?
No, people filled my rooms and stairs
For it was hear that gathered
In birth, death, song, and prayer
Yes, my walls knew happy times
And loneliness I never felt
I enjoyed the hustle and bustle of people
And the sounds they always dealt

Memories, wind-blown?
Yes, that's what I am today
The sounds have gone
So have the people, oh so far away
Gone in all directions
Will they ever return?
I hope so
It's sad to be just memories, wind-blown

People and Their Crossroads

    GLORIA GIPSON SUGGS

RALPH AND HANNAH:
KEEP THE FAMILY TOGETHER

Ralph and Hannah lived southeast of Peter and Rhea. Ralph was Peter's brother and Hannah was Rhea's sister. Ralph and Hannah had sixteen children. They were also members of Gatewood Church. Their lifestyle as farmers, was about the same as the other families in community. Ralph also grew tobacco which he tried and roll for his own chewing and smoking needs. He owned a grits mill on which he ground corn to produce meal to bake corn bread. He was a deacon of the church that met on the 1st Sunday. Hannah served on the motherboard.

They lived in a Bong-A-Low which Ralph helped build. It had a large front and porch with centered doors on the front and back. The front door opened into a hallway that had a bedroom on the left and a parlor on the right. A large dining room was off the left bedroom and a kitchen was off the dining room. His daughter Cora, a beautician, use to come out on weekends to do hair. Members of the community would line the walls in straight back chairs, waiting for her to give them the latest hair do. Later on, they built on additional room which doubled the size of this house. They decorated their yard with low growing ever greens, zinnias, and rose bushes.

Hannah died in the mid 1950s in this house, in her bedroom surrounded by her family, which included a 6 month old baby. Her funeral and burial was held at Hudsonville Church. In spite of the challenges of raising sixteen children alone, Ralph managed to keep his family together. The rose bushes Hannah planted before she died, still blooms today.

I Know About My Roses

I know about my roses
I tend them everyday
I cut out the weeds and undergrowth
So nothing is in their way

I know about my roses
I watch them one by one
I pray that God may keep them
As they go and come

I know about my roses
I count them everyday
There were sixteen when I checked last
Did one or two go away?

I know about my roses
God has blessed them one and all
I come each day in a very quiet way
Just in case they slip and fall

Ralph started hosting the family reunions at his house after his father, Jacob died. His brothers, Peter and Louis always helped in the preparations and set-ups of these festive activities which would last for 3 days. Relatives would come from Slayden, Holly Springs, Collierville, Mt. Pleasant, Chicago, Gary, Milwaukee, St. Louise, De Moines, Omaha, Oxford, and Memphis.

The reunion would be held every even year on the 4th of July weekend. One year there were over fifteen hundred people present. It was just like a community reunion. Everybody always had a good time just like they did when their father, Jacob was hosting them.

THEY KEEP COMING

They keep coming
Some by cars
Some by trains
Some in suits
And some in jeans

They keep coming
From the oceans
From the mountains
From the beaches
And from the plains

They keep coming
From the North
From the South
From the East
And from the West

They keep coming
United by coming goals and dreams
Hearing the ancestral call
To the family reunions
Grandpa, grandma, and all

Ralph and Hannah's children attended the one and two room Henry Elementary School. They attended Rust, MI, Sand Flat, and St. Mary's high schools. Some of their children continued their education in the trades, vocational schools, and colleges.

Ralph and Hannah's legacy was, "Keep the family together".

Louis and Lula:
New Meaning To A Helping Hand

Louis and Lula lived with their 8 children in a house across the way from the house of Louis' parents, Jacob and Sarah. It was a white clap board house with a tin top. It had 4 rooms; a kitchen, 2 bedrooms, and a closed in hallway. The 2 bedrooms also doubled as sitting rooms. They raised the same crops as Sarah and Jacob. Lula planted a yearly garden and belonged to the canning and quilting groups as Rhea did. Louis belonged to the same hunting as Peter. He also loved to walk. So when his brother's Peter and Ralph, started to decline in health, Louis would walk to visit each of them, once or twice daily.

I Would Help You If I Could

You move so slowly and you seem unsure
You reach for things that aren't there
Sometimes a glass or a rocking chair
You want to go home because you feel you should
I would help you if I could

You speak so softly and unsure
You call for help but no one hears
Sometimes in shouts followed by tears
You try to do things that others would
I would help you if I could

One of their daughters, Karen, became very sick and had to miss one semester of high school at St. Mary's. Peter and Rhea's children,

Jeannie and Harvester, were her first cousins who were enrolled in the same classes. They would pick up her assignments and give them to her brother, Tommy, each day. Tommy would give Karen's work to Jeannie and Harvester for them to turn it in to teachers each day. Sometimes, if Karen had questions about her work, Jeannie and Harvester would visit and assist her.

After Sarah's death they moved into the house with Jacob. They belonged to the same church as Jacob and Sarah, Gatewood Chapel, where Louis was an usher and Lula sat on the motherboard and sung in the choir. Their children went to the same schools that Peter and Rhea's children attended. Henry Elementary School, Sand Flat and St Mary's High Schools.. After high school, some of their children went on to receive training in trades and earn college degrees.

Benjamin and Victoria: That Beautiful Couple

Benjamin and Victoria lived in the Mt. Pleasant community and were members of Isom Chapel Church that they attended on 3rd Sunday of each month. Benjamin was a brother to Rachael. They lived in a one-story tall colonial white house, with large columned front and back porches, that looked like a two-story house from the Isom Road. This house had large rooms with high ceilings. The front door opened into a hallway that was flanked on the right and left by a bedroom and parlor. The dining room was straight ahead of the hallway, in the back of the house were 2 large bedrooms and a kitchen, a large porch was on the back of the house as well.

Benjamin and Victoria used to host large dinners for the congregation of their church after 3rd Sunday services and during revival week which was always held in the 3rd week of August.

This couple reinforced how people of this area should not pity themselves because of where they came from, but use the past as a challenge for the future.

With African and Seminole background under their belts, this couple concentrated on farming and crafting. Benjamin could grow anything, he developed and tested different methods of plant-growing techniques that produced prize-winning products at local fairs. He would even share his methods to others. With that being said, Benjamin was placed in the category of self-trained teacher and Victoria on the other hand created prize-winning quilts as well.

Two people of class and good upbringing, Benjamin and Victoria still stand as a representation of what is meant by the saying, "Oh, what a beautiful couple."

TJ and Beth:
Humor Will Go A Long Way

Rhea's brother, TJ, lived farther down on Isom Road, closer to highway 311 from Benjamin and Victoria. Their lifestyle was parallel to Benjamin and Victoria, but one generation removed. TJ's wife was named Beth and they had 8 children. Their first home was a 4 room tin top house with red siding. Their second home were similar to Benjamin and Victoria's. They belonged to Isom Chapel Church. Their children attended Gatewood Elementary School, and went to Sand Flat and Byhalia when they were in high school.

TJ use to go hunting with Peter's group and he always had a long tale to tell, especially about ghosts.

A Ghost Called Moe

A ghost called Moe lives in our house
He bumps coming in
He squeaks going out
Sometimes we mistake him for a mouse
Moe is a noisy ghost

A ghost called Moe moves swiftly through our house
He throws things around
He makes whirlwind sounds
Look out!
Moe is a dangerous ghost

A ghost called Moe does pranks at night
He jumps around

     GLORIA GIPSON SUGGS

And moves quickly out of sight
Sometimes he changes from dim to bright
Moe is an elusive ghost

TJ had a good sense of humor that could cheer you up if you
were feeling down.

ROBERT AND MANDAU:
THE HOSPITALITY COUPLE

Robert and Mandau lived just down the road from her parents, Martin and Rachael. Mandau was Rhea's sister. They lived in a white clap board house with a tin top. They had 10 children and attended the church in the Mt. Pleasant, called Isom Chapel.

It did not matter how small
There was still room for all

It did not matter how cold
The love inside warmed the soul

It did not matter how poor
Riches abound from giving more

It did not matter how dark the night
The lamp in the window seemed so bright

It did not matter how great
These humble dwellings kept you safe

It did not matter how long you were gone
When you came back, you were always welcomed home

Mandau was known as a good cook in the community. During the Christmas season, she would line the shelves of her "Safe" with cakes and pies. She would also bring out her homemade grape and muster dine wine jugs and sat them beside the cabinet for Santa Claus to taste on Christmas Eve. On Christmas day, she always expected Rhea and Hannah's sons to come through on their "yearly drag" to sample the contents of her safe and jugs. The "yearly drag" was a custom where Rhea and Hannah's sons would visit every house in the community to take "Santa Claus".

Robert and Mandau's out-of-town family members would also come to visit during the holidays. Robert's family would come from Ripley. Mandau's sister, Elsie, from Chicago, would stay for a week during the holidays. She would bring fashionable clothes to give as gifts to her nieces during the visit. Her sister, Dianna out of Memphis, would visit on Christmas Day. She would bring Christmas cheer in the form of food and the latest news about the social scene in Memphis. Mandau's cousin, Vera, would visit the week after Christmas. She would bring quilt patterns and cloth to give Mandau ideas of what her next quilt would look like. Rhea and her family would be there also during visits like these. Mandau and the other visitors would go piece-a-way with Rhea through the dense, back to her house.

Robert and Mandau's children attended Gatewood Elementary School, Sand Flat and Byhalia high schools. Their children continued their education in the trades, vocational schools, and colleges.

WALTER AND MARY:
WHERE COLOR DID NOT MATTER

Walter and Mary were sharecroppers who lived off Slayden Road with their 6 children on Jeremy's place. Jeremy was a land owner who lived in Slayden. This house had red brick siding and a tin top. It was just west of a large tree on Slayden road that people use to stand under while waiting on school buses or to catch rides to town. They attended a church in Slayden and their children attended the Agricultural School in Slayden.

The house they lived in had 2 bedrooms, a kitchen, and a back porch. Before they moved to this house, they lived in the house on the place that Peter and Rhea bought. Walter and Peter were childhood friends.

Walter and Mary's farm life were the same as everyone else's in the community. They did not receive special favors from any group because they were white. Walter use to say, We're "dirt poor", in reference to the fact that they did not own their own land.

They raised cotton and corn as primary crops. They also planted fruit trees around their home. During the summer, Walter would sell this fruit off the back of his black truck in Slayden for extra income.

Also during this time, Mary, just like Rhea, would take the children to hunt and gather blackberries, plums, and pork salad. She would can this food in order to have an ample supply in the fall and winter. Walter would hunt wild game and kill hogs with the other men in the community. Mary canned and/or salted down these meats for later use.

After many years of sharecropping, he was able to purchase land and build a home on it. This house was built just a few yards from the one his family lived in as sharecroppers. Their children continued their education in vocational schools and colleges.

Wayne and Emma: The Chulahoma Connection

Just west of Holly Spring, off highway 4 near the county line, lived Wayne and Ramona. They were the grandparents of Fredrick who married Jeannie, the daughter of Peter and Rhea, in the late 1960's.

This couple's lifestyle was just about parallel to that of Peter and Rhea's on the east side of Holly Springs. They were children of former slaves and knew what it meant to overcome obstacles. They married at age 15 and had 5 daughters. Wayne and Emma worked as sharecroppers until they purchased their place in the mid 1930s. Wayne was head deacon at Mt. Peal Baptist Church. He was the lead trustee of Phillip Elementary School. Emma was a member of

Chulahoma Baptist Church where she was a Sunday school teacher. She also wrote the Chulahoma news weekly and sent it to the South Reporter in Holly Springs.

Let Me Tell Your Story Today

Let me tell your story today
Straight from Lucy's corner
I give the current news
From near, far, and yonder

Let me tell your story today
Straight from Phillip's school
I discuss visitations, illnesses, and recreations
When reporting Chulahoma news

Let me tell your story today
I start with a friendly greeting
As you say it, I will send it in
Without hidden meanings

Their farm served as a backdrop for recalling many days of the past when times was hard. So they were active in the civil rights movement because they did not want that day to return.

Wayne and Emma, who were self-educated, wanted better things for their daughters. So after they completed grade school at Phillip Elementary, they sent them to boarding high schools in Hernando, Baptist Industrial High, and Holly Springs, Rust. They went on to receive teaching certificates and college degrees and taught school in the Chulahoma community. Four of their daughters moved to Chicago and Milwaukee. One remained in the Marshall County area and was a teacher in the Tate County School District.

They would all come home during the 2nd week of August to visit and attend revival at Chulahoma Baptist Church.

Wayne and Emma raised their grandson, Fredrick. He was 2 years old when his mother, their daughter -Pearl, moved to Chicago to get a job. A teacher in the 1940 did not make much, maybe a few dollars a month. Fredrick attended Phillips and Galina Elementary schools. He went to Rosenwald and Byhalia high schools. He received his college degree from Memphis State University, now U of M, in Memphis

So each year, Fredrick and Jeannie would be sure Pearl, Wayne, and Emma got a chance to go to Slayden to see Peter and Rhea.

Teachers Of Teachers And Other People

Paul and Jewel:
Supporters Of Others, Especially Children

Paul was Sarah's brother. He married Jewel who was from an adjacent county. They built their home in the late 1940's or early 1950's. It was a white clap board house with green shatters and a front porch. The large living and dining rooms were separated by paned glass doors. The walls of these 2 rooms was covered by 4-inch-wide knotted pine planked paneling. It contained a large kitchen with a sink and running water, 3 bedrooms, and a bathroom. It had a screened in back porch on the back and a single carport on the side. Green wooden shingles covered this house.

Paul and Jewel were highly educated for their day. Paul attended the Normal School that was located on Rust College campus and Jewel attended Mississippi Industrial College in Holly Springs. After completing the required courses, both of them went on to teach at the one and two room schools in the area. The core curricula at that time was reading, writing, and arithmetic.

They also worked as farmers. They did not have children of their own. They looked forward to the last two weeks of the school year when Peter and Rhea would let their children, Jeannie and Harvest spend this time with them. Jewel would be at the bus stop each day to greet them and catch up with the happenings at school. During harvest time, they use the children in the surrounding communities to help them gather their crops so they could earn money for their families. They owned a big Black Chevrolet sedan car. Paul used it to pick up and drop off the helpers. Jewel would prepare lunch each day for the workers. She became well known during that time for the butter roll pies and black-eyed peas she would serve.

They were not selfish with their success. To help others, they would pay, not barter, for work done for them. They would also make small loans but stressed the importance of meeting obligations by charging interest if late.

Paul was a Sunday school superintendent at his church which had service every first Sunday. Jewel served on the motherboard and was known for her dynamic prayers. Paul was known as an eloquent speaker and dynamic singer at conventions. Jewel was noted for her talent at training and caring for animals. She gave all of their animal's names. Only when she called them by names would the animals respond. She taught one of her dogs to sing "Nearer My God to Thee."

Paul and Jewel were examples of what people with roots just out of slavery could achieve if they wanted to.

Russell and Vera:
An Encouraging Word

Russell and Vera were members of Kimbrough Chapel, a Baptist church which held service on the 4th Sunday in each month. They attended the normal schools and received their credentials to teach in one and two room school houses in Marshall and Benton Counties. At church, Russel was the treasurer and Vera was the secretary.

Their home was built on the same style of Paul and Jewel, their friends, who lived just west of them. Their house had black shatters and black wooden shingles on the roof. They were also farmers and were very active in the civic activities.

As teachers, they loved children and always encouraged them to do their best at what they did, even at church. Children would go from church to church trying to get their nerves up to recite poems or sing songs on children's day programs. Most of the time the children would be reluctant to get up at all by the time their names were called, or they would get up when the wrong names were called. Then from the front row seat in the church, the children would hear voices saying "Come on, child. There is nothing that can go wrong when you are singing for the Lord." From the amen corner, voices would say, "That sounds mighty good." They would go from church to church giving this type of moral and spiritual support to young people.

Russell and Vera were talented in their own right. Russell's eloquent testimonials always stirred up the Holy Ghost. The children always thought Russell was a preacher because of the way he talked and dressed. Vera was considered to be nice looking and also dressed well. Just seeing them perform in public was so dynamic that if you had anything you wanted to say you would say it. If you had a song to sing, you would sing it. That was just how powerful this couple was.

They owned Atway Store on Slayden Road. They were also farmers on the land they owned around the store.

Zack: The Student
Who Could Not Read

Zack, a fifth grade student who was fifteen years old, stood six feet tall, and weighed one hundred and fifty pounds, missed school a lot. When asked by his teacher why he was absent so much, he said his father needed him to work in the fields. He was the main tractor driver for Jeremy, Peter's friend, who owned the large farm on which Zack's family lived. The teacher questioned him further by asking, "Why don't you come to school when you can? It is winter time now and you still have missed four days in a row."

Zack responded with tears in his eyes, "Well teacher, I can't read."

The teacher asked Zack, "Well, how did you make it to the 5th grade?"

He responded, "I copied the class work and tests from my sister that is also in the 5th grade. She sits in front of me in class. My daddy told me that I have to complete the 8th grade or he will stop me from driving the tractor."

The teacher called his sister to the back of the room where she was talking quietly to Zack. The teacher asked her, "How long have you known that your brother could not read."

She said, "I have known it all the time. Zack gives me money each time I help him make passing grades on his class work."

The teacher said to Zack in a stern voice, "From now own, do not copy off her work and do not pay her for helping you with your homework until she teaches you how to read."

Zack asked the teacher in astonishment, "But teacher, what am I going to do about the problem of graduating three years from now?"

The teacher answered him in the same tone of voice, "If your sister charges you enough for each reading lesson, in three years you will know how to read and also count before you graduate. Your sister will also learn that she will not get paid until she completes the

　　　　GLORIA GIPSON SUGGS

job of teaching you how to read. Most of all, your sister will learn that the dishonest act of letting you copy her work, just to earn quick money, could result in serious consequences for her."

Zack graduated from 8th grade and went on to be a straw boss on Jeremy's farm where his family lived as sharecroppers. Some years later, he attended a trade school in Memphis and became an auto mechanic. Zack always remember the teacher that taught him the real meaning of "Honesty is the best policy."

Jeannie:
The Smart Girl Who Stuttered

When Jeannie, Peter and Rhea's daughter, started school at the one room school house, she could do all written work with no problem. But, when asked to read something orally, she would hesitate. The teacher would usually call on another student because of time. At recess, Jeannie did not go outside to play with the other children. Instead, she went up to the teacher's desk and handed her a note that said, "I don't want to read out loud because I stutter so bad." The teacher told Jeannie, "The only way you will get over your stuttering is to read out loud." Jeannie replied, "But, teacher, if I read out loud, everyone will laugh at me and call me Mumbling Mosby for the rest of the day." The teacher said, "Well, Jeannie, oral reading is a major part of your daily grade, so there is no way I can let you do written work all the time. "The teacher paused for a while and asked Jeannie, "Do you sing?" Jeannie replied in a happy tone, "Yes, teacher, I love to sing when I am alone." The teacher said, "For your homework this weekend, go to a quiet place and sing your reading assignment several times aloud. Then read it aloud several times until you are comfortable with the script. Read it slowly out loud and silently. Be sure to breathe deeply as you read each line when you feel the urge to stutter. It will take a while for your confidence level to build, but just keep saying to yourself, "I can do it." Now Jeannie, go outside and play with the rest of the students. I will call on you to read your assignment first thing Monday."

The next week, Jeannie waited anxiously for the teacher to call on her to read. The teacher had the class to read the first reading together. Then, she called on Jeannie to read a shorter passage that was different from the one she was assigned. Jeannie read through the passage, hesitating twice, as if she wanted to stutter. Then, the teacher had Jeannie and the group to read a longer passage out loud together. Jeannie thought the reading class was over. So she sighed with relief and immediately proceeded to put the reading book aside. Then to her surprise, the teacher called on her to read her assigned passage. Jeannie did so to her own surprise, without a stutter.

It took Jeannie many years to overcome her chronic stuttering problem. Later on, she participated in and won several local oratorical contests. She graduates valedictorian of her 8th grade class and had to make a speech during the graduation exercise. Jeannie was always grateful to that teacher in the one room school house that taught her techniques on how to overcome obstacles and build confidence also.

Roads to St. Mary's:
Narrated by Jeannie

In the 1950s, Fr. Michael Monley, pastor and Sr. Lamana, principal contacted the parents of our community about enrolling students in St. Mary's School. Marshall County was in the process of consolidating the one and two room school houses into larger building complexes where elementary and high schools were combined in order to meet the "separate but equal" guidelines of the time in the state of Mississippi. My parents, Rhea and Peter let 9 of us attend St. Mary's during the 1950s and 60s if the bus could pick us up on Slayden Road. The walk from home to this road was 2 miles, but we did not mind because we knew the conditions of our roads during inclement weather would make it impossible for the bus to pick us up at home. Furthermore, we had to walk this distance to go Henry Elementary School. So, we did not mind walking 2 miles to go the bus stop. When the bus routes were assigned, our bus stop on Slayden Road was on the list. Mr. Henry and Mr. Jim were bus drivers on our route at that time. Because of their demands for discipline and order from students on the bus, I knew I could develop time management skills.

I enrolled at St. Mary's School in Holly Springs as a 9th grader in 1958 after graduating 8th grade as valedictorian of my class from Henry Elementary School on Slayden Road in Marshall County. The teachers during my 8th year stay at Henry were Mrs. Dunham, Mrs. Reynolds, Ms. Ford, Mrs. Plaxico, and Mrs. Cummings. They utilized various organizational skills, teaching techniques, and disciplinary styles that allowed one teacher to effectively teach all grade levels, in the same room, at the same time, 8 hours a day, for the duration of a school year. Because of these teachers, I knew I could go anywhere and do anything.

So, the elementary education I received at Henry School gave me a strong foundation to build on during my four year stay at St. Mary's.

Sr. Marianelle taught Music Appreciation, Voice and Music Lessons, and Choir. She always kept her classes interesting. I particularly enjoyed the excitement she made when she was teaching us the songs to Broadway Musicals. She taught her classes like she was preparing us for big Hollywood productions. She assigned committees to make sure everything would be ready for the big nights in Carnegie Hall at Mississippi Industrial College. She started planning all segments of each scheduled event by involving everyone from day one of each class. This made everybody feel important. So we worked hard to make sure all events were successful. Like a good teacher, she set rules, limits, and high expectations for us. Her teaching style worked because grades were calculated by a simple formula: Input = Output. I knew I could become a performer because of her classes.

Mr. Lean taught Basic English and Communication Skills. He used an individualized teaching approach where we would know if we mastered a lesson taught that day before leaving class. Attention and self-discipline were the keys to doing well in his classes. Because of Mr. Lean's classes, I knew I could talk without stuttering.

Sr. Lamana taught English Literature and Language Arts. I always enjoyed the lessons in Public Speaking and Creative Writing. Her classes brought out a competitive edge in me which made me feel like I could win any contest and achieve any goal through hard work. I knew I could be a poet and writer because of her classes.

Sr. Alexa taught Biology, Typing, Home Economics, Geometry, and Art. I liked her classes because I could use techniques learned immediately in school, home, and the community. Because of the skills I learned in her classes, people paid me to make clothes for them before and after I graduated from St. Mary's. I knew I could be an artist because of her classes.

Coach Evans taught Physical Education and Team Sports. He stressed that each student had something to contribute to a team. "If you can't make the winning shot in a game, do the supporting cheer.

If you can't run a mile in a race, walk your best yard." Because of his classes, I knew I could play a vital and supportive role in a family as a partner and parent.

Sr. Donatilla taught Chemistry, Algebra, and History. She made her history classes exciting and interesting by integrating stories of her stay in China where she spent many years in a concentration camp. I knew I could be a teacher because of her classes.

Fr. Monley taught Religion and conducted daily mass. When I converted from Baptist to the Catholic Faith, he baptized me. He conducted the wedding ceremony when I married Freddie in the late 1960's. Because of his influence in my life, I knew I could remain true to the Catholic Faith.

The roads to St. Mary's were long and sometimes rough. Fortunately, there were great people who traveled these roads with me. Their work prepared me for other roads that lead to a stronger belief in God, a desire for higher education and adventure, and the awareness that equality of human and civil rights is an inherited gift for all mankind to share. And yes, I graduated with 2 more student at valedictorian, ranked at the top of the class.

Integration of a Different Matter

In the community where Peter and Rhea lived, black and white farmers worked side by side to insure the survival, security, health, and well-fare of all people in the community. Times were hard, so team effort made the difference. But team effort, when it came to education during the years of desegregation, was a different matter.

The one and two room school houses, which were segregated and worked under the "separate but equal" concept, were closed down during the 1950s. Large school buildings that could accommodate many students and grades were built. The consolidation of these schools also meant that all student, black and white, should attend the same schools in order to satisfy the desegregation degree. This degree was handed down by the Supreme Court in the early 1950s. Well, the schools were built, but still continued to operate for a long time as "separate but equal". It was not until years later, when all segments of the desegregation process were implemented, did the public schools in the area become integrated.

All students in Peter and Rhea's community was assigned to Sand Flat School which was located west of Slayden on highway 72. It was named after the two room school Sand Flat, which was located east of Slayden on highway 72. All grade levels were eventually taught at this school.

Buses were sent to pick up all students. When the blacks were attending the one and two room schools, everybody walked to school. Some had to walk for 1 to 3 miles one way just to get there. When busing started, these same students had to walk the same distances to catch the buses at the bus stops. Some of the roads that the students lived on were impassable for buses to travel. The road crews only worked county roads.

Some people selected to send their children to both public and private schools. Peter and Rhea decided to send their children to St. Mary's, a private Catholic School that was located in Holly Springs. They did so because Sand Flat, the county school which their children were assigned, was a long time getting books and vital school supplies that were vital to the learning process. His brothers, Ralph and Louis, sent their children to Sand Flat and St. Mary's. Peter's friends, Jeremy and Walter, sent their children to The Agricultural School. It was a private school located in the town of Slayden.

Sometimes, with the blacks and whites riding different buses, things would happen to cause racism to rear its "eerie head". It all started at a bus stop down at the intersection of Slayden Road and highway 7.

A white couple enrolled their children into St. Joseph's, a white private Catholic school that was located in Holly Springs and not on St. Mary's school which was a private Catholic school for blacks. This couple had been driving their children to and from school, but found jobs in Memphis. This caused them to leave home earlier than usual in order to get to work on time. This was too early to drop their children off at St. Joseph's school. So, they made arrangements with

      GLORIA GIPSON SUGGS

the principal of St. Mary's to instruct the bus driver to pick up their children and take them to and from St. Joseph's on St. Mary's bus.

This worked well for 2 days. On the 3rd day during the drop-off of the children, the bus driver was confronted at the bus stop by 3 angry white men. They said to the bus driver, "Tell the principal that we will stop this bus from coming down this road if those white children continue to ride it. Also, tell Peter that we will be "visiting" him soon if this activity does not stop." The 3 men were upset with Peter because they had heard he was the one who signed up for this bus route. The bus driver went back to St. Mary's and relayed the message to the principal.

The next day, the principal, Sr. Mary, rode on the bus with the driver. Another car following behind to pick the white children up, just in case there was trouble. To their surprise, a neighbor of the parents of the children came over to the bus stop. He told the principal who were standing outside of the bus with the driver that the family had moved back to Memphis. So he did not have to transport them anymore. The principal got back on the bus and sighed with relief. She rode the bus for the complete route. The car behind the bus continued to follow the route. It contained 2 undercover police officers who were trained in crisis intervention. The principal had contacted them the night before.

On the route back, she got off the bus at Peter's children's bus stop and instructed the bus driver to go on back to school. She got in the car with the 2 officers and directed them to take her to Peter's house so she could alert him of the threat that was made towards him by the three white men the day before. Peter had already heard of the incident from his children but still had a high level of concern about it. The officers gave him their contact information, just in case something else came up concerning this matter. Nothing else ever did. No one ever came forth to identify the 3 angry white men who upset racial relations in the community that day.

Over time, the community settled down into a somewhat normal routine. And Peter, Rhea, and their family continued to be very active in the Civil Rights' movement. Their sons Ben, Mark, and Stetson worked with this movement during and after the 1960s. They traveled extensively throughout Mississippi, encouraging people to register and vote. Peter participated in the March on Washington in the 1960s. Benjamin and Stetson help to set up the Head Start programs in this community. Later on, a Head Start Center in Mt. Pleasant, MS was named in Honor of Benjamin. Their daughter, Frenchie, was the first black librarian at the Marshall County Library in Holly Springs.

Peter and Rhea's family was also involved in defending their country. Peter served military duty during World War II in the Navy. Their sons Benjamin and Mark served in the Army during the Korean Conflict, and Boone served in the Army during the Vietnam War. His son-in-law, Fredrick, Jeannie's husband, served in the Air Force in the Vietnam War.

Fun Times

Timothy and Sylvia: A Teacher And The Picnic Man's Call To Play Ball

Sylvia was a school teacher in the community for three generations. Timothy was known for his skills in planning and executing recreational events such as picnics and fish fries. They were members of Hudsonville church.

Sylvia taught in a one room school house that was up the road from their home called Henry Elementary. She was one of Peter's teachers when he attended Atway Elementary. Rhea attended Gatewood Elementary School in the Isom community. The small one school was big enough to house all eight grades. The curriculum at that time was mainly reading, writing, and arithmetic. Sylvia used teaching techniques that included peer tutoring, group work, spelling bees, and singing. Sylvia's teaching methods helped to prepare the students for participation in debates, oratorical contests, and plays.

School was held in split sessions: periods between fall and winter and summer and fall when crops were not being planted, cultivated, or harvested. People who were sharecroppers were sometimes unable to attend school if late crops were produced. So sometimes teachers, such as Sylvia, taught reading, writing, and arithmetic in their homes to make up for lost time. These split sessions may have discouraged many students from attending school because of the long breaks in the learning process.

Timothy played a major role in building the social structure of the community. He would manage a major picnic each year in a central location, usually in a field just north and south of the one room school. Large crowds would always come because of the variety of what was offered: games, plenty of food and drinks, games and rides for the children. His picnics seemed like carnivals, bazaar, and dance halls, all rolled up into one big package to the children. You could buy a fish sandwich and a drink for a quarter. That left about $0.75 to spend on other activities.

He would get a lady called Clara, who lived on Jeremy's place off north Slayden Road, to fry the fish. Clara took fish frying seriously. So, in order to meet her request, Martin would set up a #30 wash pot on an iron tripod for her to use. He would stack a pile of thinly cut fire wood in easy reach of her pot setup. He would also bring her a large can of HUMCO Lard, loaves of bread, and jars of mayonnaise, mustard, and pickle relish. And yes, for Clara to fry, Martin would bring pounds of buffalo, catfish, and flounder. She always brought her own yellow meal, salt, and black pepper to make the fish batter and utensils. As a sure money maker, Martin would sat Clara up at the front of the line of picnic vendors on left side of the picnic ground entrance.

The main attraction at this and other picnics in the community, was baseball. Rhea and Peter's son, Mark was the manager of a team called the Atway Rockets. He would go to other games in the Slayton area, looking for players to enhance this well-known and established team.

He found a left handed pitcher, named, Sticks. Sticks was the grandson of Timothy and Sylvia. He lived with his parents, Bob and Mamie, just north of Slayden off highway 72. Bob, a son of Timothy and Sylvia owned land and lived in a three room house with a front and back porch. Sticks was a student at Sand Flat Elementary School.

Mark picked his brother, Harvester, also known as Hot, as catcher and pitcher. He selected his 1st cousin, Mathew, one of Hannah and Ralph's sons, to be an outfielder. Mathew, because he was such a good outfielder, was invited twice, by the Dodgers, to attend their summer camp. They had hoped he would be selected to play on their team. Mathew had to pass up the chance to play with the Dodgers because he did not have money to pay his way to the camp. So he played his best with the Atway Rocks. He had a cool, laid back style of play that drew large crowds because he was wanted by the Dodgers.

The Sand Flat Choppers, a team managed by a man named Shelton, came to the picnic to play against the Rockets. This team was from the Roberts Chapel and Corn Cord Church communities, located just north of Slayden. The game was in the last inning, with all bases loaded, and scores tied. The pitcher named "Hot" was called to play. Hot was a 6 ft. tall pitcher who was known to put on a good show at the pitcher's mound. He got the nickname Hot because he threw each ball with lighting speed. It seemed if each ball was on fire and he had to get rid of it before it burned his hands. This day, Hot gave the crowd what they wanted: a strike out, which placed the game into extra innings. Both teams agreed to play innings until a winner was declared.

Mark and Shelton, the teams' managers, went over to talk to Timothy, the picnic organizer, about setting up lights on the field. Timothy did so immediately.

The Choppers went to home position to bat. Martin put Sticks in as pitcher, Hot as catcher, and Mathew as outfielder between 2nd and 3rd base.

When Sticks took his position on the pitcher's mound, it became obvious why he was named "Sticks". He was 6ft and 2in tall with a thin frame. While throwing the ball, he would turn his body real fast in circular motions. This action produce the illusion of Sticks spending around on the ground which would also distract the batters. He would through the ball at lightning speed.

The first batter up struck out. The next batter had watched Sticks movements. He thought he had figured out the rhythm of Sticks throw arm. He hit the ball way out between 2nd and 3rd base right into the mitten of Mathew. The 2nd out was called by the empire. Then the Choppers sent a short muscular player called Mike, to bat. Sticks threw his fast ball at the right angle to Mike's bat which produced a home run.

The 3rd play up to bat. Strike one, strike two, and strike three were called for the 3rd out for the Choppers

Now the Rockets was up for bat. Sticks hit his 2nd ball and made it to 2nd base. Hot hit his 1st ball and made it to 2nd with Sticks moving into home, making the score 1:1. Mathew moved to the plate. First ball he struck out. But he hit the 2nd ball so far out until it could not be found. So, it was declared a home run. The game ended 1:3 in favor of the Rockets.

Timothy would start a picnic at 6 am on Saturday morning and end it at midnight. He would be sure the picnic site was cleaned up and cleared of people before leaving the grounds.

On Sundays at church, Timothy would sell softdrinks, candy, and sandwiches out of the back of his black truck, if some special event such as a children's day program, was going on.

The echo of the school bell and the call to "play ball" can still be heard because of Sylvia and Timothy.

THAT FISHING POND

Let's get our canes at just about dawn
And go down to that fishing pond

We'll leave the fields when the work is done
And catch some fish from that fishing pond

The adults won't mind, the cool winds have come
They might go with us to that fishing pond

Let's be real quiet and place our hooks toward the sun
So we'll catch plenty of fish from that fishing pond

   GLORIA GIPSON SUGGS

LUKE: THE HUNTER AND CARPENTER

Luke was a land owner and fascinating character in the community. His family's property was located adjacent to Jacob and Sarah's property. He was tall, dark, and lean in build. He always had a pipe in his mouth and a shot gun on his saddle. He wore well-polished boots and road a groomed reddish brown horse that strutted with pride.

Luke would visit every week to update everyone on his hunting successes or failures. He hunted raccoons, rabbits, and squirrels in the winter. During late fall and early spring, he hunted birds and ducks.

Sometimes he hunted with other men, especially at night. Luke would usually organize these large hunts which took place over a period of several days at a time. Whatever bounty that was killed was always disturbed equally among the party. They usually hunted over an area of 600 acres which extended from Hudsonville Depot to Slayden and Mt. Pleasant.

Luke was a self-taught carpenter that help to build, expand, and repair most of the homes in this community. He never used blueprints. He also would help cut the trees and set up a saw mill to produce the planks for the houses he would work on. You only had to tell him what you wanted done and he would do it to your specifications if possible.

The aroma from his pipe always alerted the children of his presence if he were not seen or heard riding up. During his visits, he would tell jokes and tales of folks and events that he found interesting.

TELL ABOUT THAT HONKY-TONK

Once there was a Honky-tonk
Way back off the road
It was a different kind of Honky-tonk
At least that's what was told
People came to this Honky-tonk
Just to have fun
On Friday right a sundown
That Honky-tonk was always full

There was always dancing at that Honky-tonk
To Blues, Country, and Rock-n-Roll
The Twist, the Square Dance, the Electric-Slide
Some even danced the Stroll

The fish fries started at sun down
They fried Salmon-Catfish-Perch
Whiten-Buffalo-and Trout
That fish tasted so good

Some people called it a night spot
And some called it a country club
As imagined by a child-some will agree
That was a special kind of Hunky-tonk

                    GLORIA GIPSON SUGGS

Christmas with Little Willie
and the Five Keys

During the 1950's, a band with Rhythm, Blues and Rock and Roll sound was formed. It was called Little Willie and the Five Keys. The band members were from Holly Springs and attended St. Mary's and Rosenwald schools. It was a popular band that played at most of the dances and proms in the Holly Springs area. This band was regularly booked to play at activities throughout the southeast because of its "crossover appeal" sound.

Peter and Rhea's daughter, Jeannie, talked to the students on her bus route about having a Christmas party and dance. She stated that her parents had agreed that it could be held at their home, but only if the other students' parents attend. She mentioned that it would be "Pot Luck" and held on the 2nd day of Christmas, December 26, 1960. She asked them to think about it, discuss it with their parents, and let her know the next day.

The next day, it was unanimous. All students and parents wanted to come. At school, during homeroom, Jeannie mentioned the party to her classmate, Warren, a member of Five Keys. Warren asked Jeannie, "How would you like for the band to play at the party? We would not charge anything." And furthermore, Warren and Alford, two other students in this class, are also members of the band. Jeannie was so surprise at Warren's request until she shouted, "yes" out loud during homeroom. So, to calm the curiosity of her classmates, she extended the same invitation to the party to them.

By homeroom the next day, Jeannie's party list was conformed. She and her family had 2 weeks, the Christmas break, to prepare for the party.

And what a party they had. A line of cars and pick-ups trucks drove in at about the same time. They filled up all yard space and the road on both sides leading down to the house. Students and parents filed in with food and drinks. The furniture in all rooms downstairs had been moved aside. The parents setup in the dining room and spent time visiting and getting to know each other. They also assisted with the serving of food and drinks. Some of them joined in with the dancing when the band started playing.

The band setup in a corner on the west side of the living room next to the fireplace. The living room, hallway, front and back porches were used for dancing. And did the band play? It played everything from Sam Cook's version of "Born by the river" to Elvis Presleys "I'm Dreaming of a White Christmas". And did the students dance? They danced everything from the "Stroll" to the "Waltz". Everybody, including the parents, had a mighty good time that day on December 26, 1960.

Scary and Bold Times

HENRY: THE SNAKE CATCHER

Henry was loved and feared by many in the community. He ran away from home at an early age to join the circus. This was his training ground for the daring tricks he performed after he returned home as an adult; the practice of charming and catching snakes.

When Henry would show up at a picnic or other outside gatherings, all would be well. He would go around and greet everyone just like the other people there would do. Usually, Henry was a quiet, well-mannered guy that stood 6ft. tall. He was a sharecropper who lived in a house on Jeremy's place not too far from Slayden. He was one of the main tractor and truck drivers for Jeremy during the peak seasons for planting and gathering cotton. He would be one of the first people the show up to help other farmers if they needed him when he was not working for Jeremy. Ordinarily, Henry was a well-liked guy.

And then, during the late fall after, Henry's behavior would change. He would show up at these festive activities and then disappear for several hours into the deep surrounds. Most of the people gathered would sigh with relief, thinking Henry had gone home for the day. Then, right a sun down, Henry would show up again to the crowds dismay. Slowly, he would move slowly through the crowd causing then to scatter in horror, because of what they saw; 5 or 6 snakes coiled around his neck. Little did the crowd know that he had defanged the snakes before he adorned himself with them in public. This would break the activity up for the day.

These displays of Henry's were expected to happen at every gathering if he were there. If the children saw him, they knew that sooner or later it would happen. The moment of surprise was so frightening that tears would come from the children's eyes just because they saw him. The parents usually would take the kids away for fear they would be overcome with fear. A group of men would usually scold Henry, as if that was going to stop him. The sheriff was notified before each activity but he could never catch him doing it. Over the years, these activities of Henry slowed down. But, at each festival event, the children knew that sooner or later, Henry would surely do it again.

Sometimes other men would dare him to do it. Then, sometimes it seemed as if it was the dare or mystery from the reptiles' hisses that led him to this type of behavior.

The Dogs Howled All Night

The dogs howled all night
That far long night in July
We shiver at the thought of it
That sound that made us cry

Far west in the distance
That sound that broke our sleep
One howl, one continuous howl
We prayed to the Lord our soul do keep

What deathly sound, what piercing sound
Came in the dark of night
The sound may stop and calm our fears
Just at the break of light

Narrow Escape:
A moment of danger

Yes, it is wonderful to find myself living and moving about after a close call with death in the early 1950s. It is strange, though, how I took life for granted up until that time.

It was on a September day when I, along with other family members, was coming home from gathering cotton in a faraway field. It was dusk dark and everyone was tired.

I was sitting on the passenger side of the truck, next to the door, trying to make myself comfortable from a long day of picking cotton. As I did, the door of the moving truck came open and I fell out. I passed out just for a moment, one long moment. And in that moment, I saw complete darkness.

Unaware of what had happened, I woke up on the ground and found myself under the truck, next to the back wheels. I was surrounded by crying and concerned family members and the driver, LQ. They thought I was dead. But thanks to a quick reacting driver, I came out of it all with just an injured knee.

Now, sometimes during quiet moments, my mind drifts back to that scene in the 1950s. And again, I am able to witness that unforgettable narrow escape.

You Are Gonna Get a Whoppin' for That

You stole watermelons from your great-uncle's patch.
You broke a windowpane and you didn't put it back.
You let the cows get out and the hogs are not fat.
You are gonna get a whoppin' for that.

     GLORIA GIPSON SUGGS

You visited all day instead of working till dawn.
You played every game when the adults were gone.
You rode the horse too fast and you drenched the cat.
You are gonna get a whoppin' for that.

You didn't wash the dishes or clean the house.
You forgot to get the eggs from the hayloft out
You put on your Sunday clothes-shoes and hat.
You are gonna get a whoppin' for that.

Questionable and Uncertain Feelings

Who Sees the Beauty?

Who sees the beauty of nature?
Is it the person who walks by moonlight
in a trance defined as love?
Is it the child who feels its mother's tears
warm against its cheeks?
Or could it be the blind man who
captures the glow of the sun in a dream?
And hears the gushing of a wind-blown lake?

Who sees the beauty of nature?
Are there special beings who have been
endowed with this rare gift?
Or is this rare gift something that has
been instilled in all living things?
Who amongst us can really testify to the depth
and warmth of nature's rare beauty?
And reveal to all the hidden secrets of it

Life's Ups and Downs

I have difficulty understanding life
Things and people are always moving so fast
And sometimes things hurt so deeply

In figuring out life, I place things such as hate, despair,
Love, pain, and patience at the top of my list
Because these are the most difficult for me to understand

But problems are solved everyday
So why these things can't be understood by me?
I know they can be solved, but how?

A Child in Despair

I can't go on like this
All weighted down with problems
Not knowing how I will make it from day to day
I have thought about running away
But where would I go?
Who would I call once I get there?

I can't go on anymore
Nothing I do is right
When I laugh, it is always too loud
When I talk, it is always in the wrong tone of voice
I can't go on anymore
I feel like a stranger lost in a crowd

We Did Not Know You

We did not know much about you
We wish we had
We used to come and visit
And relate the past

We did not see you everyday
We missed you so
We heard many things about you
We loved you so

We did not listen
You tried to tell
Why we resembled you
And you always wished us well

GLORIA GIPSON SUGGS

The Depot, Country Stores, and Experimental Farm

THE DEPOT

Hudsonville Depot was a buzzing place during the 1930s and 40's. Its location was surrounded by highway 113 on the east and highway 7 on the west. These main highways were shadowed by the Illinois Central Road that connected up to highway 78 to the north and highway 72 to the south and other highways and roads in between. This depot had a train station, storage houses, post office, and stores. The local merchants use to line up at the depot in their vehicles and wagons to buy supplies for restocking their stores with goods brought in by trains or wholesale trucks. Or they would go to the warehouses and pick up goods for restocking. It did not matter

     GLORIA GIPSON SUGGS

what day you came to the train station, it was always busy during these years.

A large number of people were migrating up north and out east in search of better jobs and lifestyle. There was also a large group that would catch the train here to go on vacations and to attend recreational and business activities, especially during the summer and winter months. Jacob and Ruth, Peter's parents, would go to the Depot during the summer so Ruth could catch the train to St. Louis to visit Elizabeth, their daughter. Ruth would stay up there for a week. She would return home with examples of the latest fashions and current news of what was going on in Elizabeth's family.

Peter and Rhea's son, Peter Jr., who lived in Gary, Indiana, use to ride the train to the Memphis train station, but only if he were having trouble with his 1952 black Pontiac sudan. His mother, Rhea would catch the train in Memphis to visit him in Gary during July each summer.

You could buy anything at the stores that you needed or wanted at Hudsonville Depot. They had a general store that carried clothes, shoes, jewelry, medication, food, and household items. The hardware store carried tools, fuel, and farming equipment. If you needed something that the store did not have, the owner would specially order it for you. He would send you a message, as soon as it came in, by mail, a carrier, or by phone, if you had a phone at that time.

Time to Catch that Train

Lend me some money to buy a ticket
I'll pay you back next week
My son is going to Chicago
The train is leaving at eight

His bags are packed and ready
To catch a ride to town
He worked in the fields yesterday
Until about sundown

Don't worry about your money
He will send it to me soon
He has a job waiting in Chicago
He got the news at noon

He will stay with relatives in Chicago
Just outside of Champaign
They will be moving back home next year
On that south-bound train

The post office was also busy. People were coming in daily to mail out packages of can goods from the their harvest to love ones who had move away and still longed for the good food they enjoyed back home. The locals would always be excited to hear about what was going on in the big cities. They would receive information about jobs and places to stay, if they wanted to come to the 'Big City".

The main post office for this area was just several miles east of the depot in a town called Lamar. It was located between highway 7 and highway 113. The mail man would go out in a black pickup truck to deliver and pick up mail on rural routes daily. If you did not have a stamp, you could leave the money in the mailbox. The mailman would stamp the letter for you and return the change, if necessary. Packages had to be brought in for mailing at the post office. But, if the mailman had his scales with him, those would also be picked up at the mailbox. The mailboxes on these rural routes were located, in some cased, a mile or more from the people's homes. The people did not mind because the mail were their only way of keeping in touch with what was going on outside the community.

Go Meet the Mail Man

Let me rest please
I am so tired
I have walked two miles to this road
I don't think the mail man has run yet
I would have heard his Model T Ford

Let me sit by the road, please
If the mail man comes, I will flag him down
I guess he will get here by noon
If he does, I can get home by one
He should be coming soon

Atway Store was located at the intersections of Atway, Kimbrough, and Slayden Road. It was a wooden store that sat upon a high bank. It had army green plank siding, a high pitched roof, and a door in the center. A tall wooden stoop with wide steps lead up to the door which was facing south. Two Esso; fuel pumps which contained gas for the cars and trucks and diesel for the tractors and wholesale trucks. The west side of the store had water and feeding troughs and hitching posts for the mules and horses of customers who traveled by wagon or horseback.

The inside of the store had a wide planked wooden floor and a wood burning pot-bellied heater that was vented through a chimney on the north side of the store.

Atway Store was a country general store that stocked food, farming and school supplies, and tool like Golden Rules in Holly Springs but on a smaller scale.

People in the community could walk to this store, if they had to, after hours if they had an emergency that could not wait until store hours the next day. The owner, Russell and Vera, lived just back of the store. All the customers had to do were to knock on their door and let them know what they needed. They would be let in the store to shop, even after midnight. Peter and Rhea, who had seventeen children, lived about 3 miles from this store. They were regular customers at this store many times due to emergencies.

ATWAY STORE

Atway store
Don't close your door
We like your wood-burning heater
And hardwood floor

Atway store
Don't turn off your light
We want to see the throughway
And the turn to the right

Atway store
Don't ran out of stock
We need softdrinks, candy
And a pair of cotton socks

Russell and Vera owned and farmed the land around this store. They also were teachers at Atway and Sand Flat Schools. Atway Elementary was located just down the road from their store. Sand Flat School was located on highway 72, east of Slayden.

The Experimental Farm

The Experimental Farm was located on highway 7 just north of Holly Springs. It was run by the United States Department of Agriculture. It consisted of a main brown brick building, 6 framed clap board house like buildings, and 5 large cement brick silos. They owned or leased hundreds of acres of land around this farm to help meet the goals of implementing research programs and developing techniques that would help farmers in the management, production, and control of grasslands, row crops, forestry, land erosion, livestock, poultry, financial assistance, and housing.

The farm agents would schedule an "on the site" visit with farmers or they could come to the Experimental Farm for help concerning their special needs. Demonstrations or workshops were also given throughout the year for homemakers on topics such as canning techniques, food preparation, and house whole pest control.

Peter and Rhea use to sign up for on-site visits and workshops at the farm. Rhea use to enjoy attending the workshops on food preparation and canning. The pressure cooker was a useful but potentially dangerous utensil. So she would learn how to use it correctly at the experimental farm and schedule demonstrations at her home for the women in her community who could not attend these workshops.

The home demonstration agent, Lucy, use to come out to Rhea's home to get updated on follow-up community activities from the classes attended at the center. After their meeting, Rhea would show off her daughters' work. Frenchie, a member of 4H Club, specialized in crochet, embroidery, and quilt piecing. Natalie liked to quilt, embroider, and sew. Laura liked to can using the latest pressure cooker techniques. Jeannie learn techniques in embroidery, sewing, and fabric painting. The twins, Eva and Reva, worked with embroidery and quilt piecing. Sarah Rachael specialized in sewing, quilting, and canning.

Peter would tell how he taught his sons, Elson, Stetson, Harvester, Boone, and JC, how to use sea grass cords to replace bottoms in straight back chairs that use to have slats. He also would show off the artwork JC had done.

Bob, the FHA agent, would come to visit with Peter every other month. They would ride over the farm in Bob's Black Chevrolet pickup truck. He would check on the new techniques Peter and his sons used to set out pine plants, rotate crops, and control soil erosion. He would also discuss how the Red Case tractor that Peter purchased through the FHA, could be used more effectively when implementing new farm techniques.

It Was All About Cotton

Cotton continued to be the major crop in the Slayden community through the 1930s, 40s, and 50s. Most farmers like Peter and Rhea, were planting and cultivating cotton with mule drawn plows, chopping it with hoes, and picking it by hand.

The 4th of July was the time they wanted their crops "turned by". This meant the last cultivation of the cotton fields in an effort to clear the fields of remaining grass that would interfere with the picking process in the Fall. Thanksgiving was the deadline they set for the picking of cotton.

THE CHOPPERS

So during May and June, all cotton fields were lined with people chopping cotton. Peter and Rhea's family would make this task fun by using a rhythmic movement of their bodies that produced synchronized sounds from their hoes. Sometimes they would sing and chop to the words of Old McDonald Had a Farm or some other spirited song.

Old McDonald had a farm,
Ee I ee I oh!
And on that farm he had some ducks,
Ee I ee I oh!
With a quack-quack here
And a quack- quack there

Here a quack, there a quack,
Everywhere a quack- quack
Old McDonald had a farm
Ee I ee I oh!

Whatever songs and rhythm styles they used, this like moved like a performing choir during the chopping process, in an effort to meet the deadline of July 4th.

THE PICKERS

Now, picking cotton by hand was a different matter. The pickers took a quiet, competitive approach to the process.

Reflections in the Field

To get the picking process in full action mode, Peter would start a contest. He would say, "I will give $5.00 to each person who picks 200 lbs of cotton by the end of the day." He would specify "cotton" because he wanted clean bags of cotton, free of debris, brought to the scales for weighing in order to reach 200 lbs. He would go on to say "No cheating allowed." So, all pickers would go into quiet mode with one goal in mind, to win the race.

Pick that cotton
Put it in the sack
Grab it fast
Bend your back
There is a race going on
Don't you want to win?
Can't you hear that cotton gin?

Five dollars to the winner
At the end of the day
For two hundred pounds gathered
What did you say?
You can spend it in town
For thread, cloth, paper, and pens
Can't you hear that cotton gin?

Peter had one goal in mind also, to clear the fields of cotton by Thanksgiving. Most of the time these goals were reached. If Peter did not reach his goals completing chopping by the 4th of July and picking by Thanksgiving, he would call in neighboring families to help him.

Bales of cotton, usually 2 at a time, were carried by wagons and trucks to the gin in Slayden or Mt. Pleasant. During this season you could hear the sounds of the gin's engines knocking for miles. They would also signal to the nearby farmers that the cotton picking season was in full bloom. Trucks and wagons would line all roads leading to these gins during the peak season of picking cotton. highways, 311, 72, 7, and Slayden Road would literally have traffic jams during this time.

Put Away the Hoes and Sacks

During the 1960s, the farmers started using herbicides to get rid of the weeds and eliminated the need for cotton choppers. So, the farmers started using their hoes to chop their truck patches and gardens. Large mechanized cotton pickers replaced the pickers. Sometimes, human pickers were called to "clean up" the cotton left behind by the cotton picking machines.

When Peter and Rhea's farm became mechanized, they assigned their son, Ben, to conduct its day to day operations. Ben went to Henry Elementary, Rust High School, and MI College. He also served in the Korean Conflict for 2 years.

It's Church Time

 GLORIA GIPSON SUGGS

Gatewood Missionary Baptist Church

Gatewood Chapel was the church to belong to in its time. People would come from far and near just to be present during one of its Sunday morning services the 1st Sunday of each month. It held its revival during the 1st week of August each year.

Gatewood Chapel was built shortly after the Civil War. It was located due west of Peter and Rhea's house on Moscow Road which was later named Slayden Road. It was attended by white people of different denominations. Henry Elementary one room school was located up the hill from the church. The cemetery was located on the southwest side. In the 1930s, most of the white families that lived in this area moved to Holly Springs, Mt. Pleasant, Collierville, and other surrounding towns.

The blacks in the community started using Gatewood Chapel in the 1930s. They made a "Life Time Estate" ownership agreement with the owner which stated: They could use the church, school, plus the 2 acres around them for as long as they wanted to, but they could never own the property or the cemetery located on it.

Jacob was named head deacon and Sarah was the lead sister of the motherboard during the 1930s when Gatewood Chapel changed over to an all-black church. Before this time, the members use to attend the church with white people or they would hold services at their homes.

Paul, Peter's uncle, was the Sunday school teacher and superintendent at Gatewood Chapel. He would start classes promptly at 9 o'clock. Everybody would be there on time for roll call. The children would really be excited because they knew Paul was going to call each of them, by name, to participate in the lesson. If you did not get a chance to read, he would ask you to act as a helper for the secretary or treasurer.

Gatewood Chapel's choir consisted of young and older members. Rhea and Peter's daughter, Sarah Rachael, directed the choir and played the piano; Timothy and Sylvia's granddaughter, Bella, was also director and leader; and Louis and Lula's daughter, Helen, sung lead. Peter and Rhea's son, Mark, had formed a quartet called the Gatewood Witnesses.

Regular service would always start at 11 o'clock. The preacher, Rev. Walker, would drive all the way from Collierville. He was a popular preacher and usually had to go to another church after leaving Gatewood Chapel. So the head usher, Louis and the other ushers, would be sure that everyone was seated or in place when Rev. Walker arrived. His wife, Mable, would be with him. She was a tall well-dressed lady that always sat on the left side of the church with the motherboard. Rev. Walker was nice looking and had a good voice. He usually would sing songs throughout his sermons because he knew singing was his strongest suit. After the devotion, he would always sing;

Lord, I stretch my hands to thee,
No other help I know
If Thy withdraw Thy Self from me
Whether shall I go?

Well, with several verses of this song, sung in a high tenor voice, I think you get the picture. All ushers, for the rest of the service, would stay busy.

One of Peter's sons, Mark, invited a great evangelist from Memphis, Rev. Wesley to come to Gatewood Chapel to preach on an evening program. Everyone had heard him preach on the radio every Sunday. He was a well-liked and famous preacher. So, Mark and the other deacons expected a large crowd. Well, a large crowd came. The church was packed wall to wall with people. People were all outside, looking and listening through the raised tall windows, just to hear Rev. Wesley. Walter and Mary, the white people who lived east of the church, also stood outside to hear him.

So the church was packed when Rev. Wesley, with his manager, Daniel, by his side, was lead in by the ushers. After the devotion, Daniel was asked to introduce Rev. Wesley to the congregation. Daniel stood up and said in a commanding voice, "Rev. Wesley will not preach tonight unless you all raise $200". Well, $200 back then was just like asking for $2,000. So, Mark directed the ushers to pass the collection plates around, inside and outside. After the count, they were short of $200.

Mark went over and talked to his grandfather, Jacob, who left the church immediately with his grandson, Little Jacob. Little Jacob, Ralph's son, drove the truck for Jacob and assisted him walking long distance. Jacob had started getting cataract on his eyes during this time.

Mark informed Daniel that the church was just short of the $200 dollars requested. Mark went on to tell the manager that his grandfather, Jacob, had gone home to get the rest of the money. He also said that it was going to take a while for Jacob to get back. There had come up a big storm the day before. So, Mark knew that Jacob would instruct Little Jacob, the driver of the truck, to go the long way around to his house. They would take Slayden Road pass Atway Store onto Atway Road, which was about 4 miles from Gatewood Church. This was done to avoid the rougher dirt roads on the shorter route which was about 2 miles.

So, to pass the time, Mark called on Sarah, a heavy sat lady that was married to his brother, Benjamin, at that time, to come up and sing a solo. She had the same name as Peter's mother. Sarah was a lyrics soprano who sang with the world renowned Rust College Acapella Choir. She sung;

Nearer, My God to Thee

Nearer, my God to Thee!
Nearer, to Thee!
E'en tho it be a cross
That rais-eth me!
Still all my song shall be!

Near-er, My God, to Thee!
Near-er, my God, to Thee!
Near-er to Thee!

The church was on fire, indoors and out, after Eva completed singing ever verse of this song. Mark saw that his grandfather had not returned with rest of the money. He went up to the pulpit to speak to the manager. Before he could do so, Rev. Wesley jump up from his seat and said, "Your money is good with me. After hearing Sr. Eva sing, I am so filled with the Holy Ghost. Just count this sermon on me."

Rev. Wesley delivered what the crowd came to hear. And Jacob returned with the rest of the $200 which was offered to Rev. Wesley at the end of the service. Rev. Wesley did not take the money. The deacons asked him why he would not take the money. Rev. Wesley said in a quiet voice, "I learned, tonight, that sometimes a fee can be paid in more forms than money. The spirit of God was in this church tonight. I felt it all down in my soul. So, that fee enough for me." After that night, Mark and the other deacons, would always ask about fees when inviting well known preachers and quartets to Gatewood Chapel.

For many years, the people in the community talked about the night when the famous evangelist and the renowned soprano came to Gatewood Chapel.

The Marshall County Health Department administered vaccination shots to people of the community at Gatewood Chapel during the1940s-50s. The Mount Pleasant ICS Head Start Program was housed at Gatewood Chapel from the 1960s through the 70s. This center, which was moved to the city of Mt. Pleasant, has been named in honor of Peter and Rhea's oldest son, Benjamin.

Hudsonville Christian Methodist Episcopal Church

Hudsonville CME Church services was always held on the 2nd Sunday in each month. They held their revival during the 2nd week of August every year. This church always attracted large crowds because of the spirited pastors the members would elect at the conventions. Rev. Jackson, a pastor from Holly Springs, pastured Hudsonville in the early 1950s. He later became an elder and bishop in the Methodist Church. When he was the pastor at Hudsonville, he was just known as Rev. Jackson.

He was a well-trained and seasoned pastor when he came to Hudsonville. He had a degree in Theology and had pastured at well-known churches in surround areas and beyond. Everybody knew he would be "moving up", the 1st day he showed up at Hudsonville. Besides having many credentials and a well-polished air, Rev. Jackson was a down to earth preacher. He always delivered spirited, well planned sermons that grew large crowds to Hudsonville for regular service and funerals. He delivered the words of each of his sermons in the same tempo that the ole spirituals were sung: Starting slow and moving to faster graduation. He also integrated a humming sound that sat the church on fire by the end of it.

This church was also known for having good singers. Barbara, a mid-wife, lived northwest of the church and sat on the motherboard. She would lead songs during the devotional part of service. She would also sing solos at funerals, if requested.

A Song Leader Called Sang

She was tall and large in structure
To some she looked rather plain
She sung in a deep voice
She never got hoarse
A song leader called Sang

She led songs that everyone knew
They all had standard refrains
A favorite song
That was not too long
 Lead by a song leader called Sang

She would stop and drink some water
From a jug next to the pew
She would pick the song up
At the right verse
That song leader everybody knew

No one knew much about her
Or the place from which she came
But they remember the words
And the contralto voice heard
From the song leader called Sang

Hudsonville was also known to have good choirs and quartets. Calvin, Rhea's first cousin, had a high tenor voice. He sung in the choir and was the main leader in the male quartet. As a soloist, Calvin would always sing acapella. He use to turn the house out by singing Amazing Grace in English. He would turn it out again by singing every verse in Swahili.

Amazing Grace

Amazing grace how sweet the sound
That saved a wretch like me!
I once was lost but now am found,
Was blind but now I see

The earlier musicians that played piano for Hudsonville and surrounding churches usually played by ear or while they were taking lessons. Later on, these churches were able to pay professional musicians. But the ones who played by ear would always do a good job. The earlier musicians usually played for the four churches in the area. They would practice with the choirs on Wednesdays or Thursdays before the service Sunday for each church. Rhea's first cousin son, Floyd, who lived on Kimbrough Road just west of the church, were one of these earlier musicians.

LET THE PIANO MAN PLAY

Let the piano man play those songs
Let the piano man play
Although a little of key
They don't sound so bad
They make the spirit come over me
Let the piano man play

Sometimes he plays different sounds
A little jazz-a little rock
You might hear some blues
But when you hear those gospel notes
You will feel the Holy Ghost
Let the piano man play

He gets up and struts around
He sits down-he stands up
Then he sits back down and plays
He sings good too
Let the spirit have its way
Let the piano man play

Hudsonville Church use to host the Methodist Convention from time to time. Peter's first cousin, JJ, use to come up from Oxford for these conventions. JJ was known for his dynamic speaking style. So, he was invited to speak often at these activities. His family was from the Hudsonville Depot area and use to belong to Graves Chapel CME Church before moving to Oxford. Graves Chapel was located south of highway 7.

Isom Chapel CME Church

I som Chapel's first church services were held under a grove of trees called a tree harbor in the Summer time. In the winter, the services would be held at member's houses. Isom Chapel's first building was erected in the late 1940's on Isom Chapel Road. This church was a sister church to Hudsonville and followed the same methodology. It was located on Isom Chapel Road in the Mt. Pleasant community and held service on the 3rd Sunday of each month. It held revival services each year during the third week in August. A small house next to the church was converted into a school house called Gatewood Elementary.

Ernie Jr., the first black mayor of Holly Springs, taught at this school. Eddie were Rhea's second cousins. Ernie Sr. and Martin were first cousins.

Rhea's sister, Mandau, her husband, Robert and their children belonged to Isom Chapel. Their parents, Martin and Rachael were members here also. Rachael and Mandau were stewardesses and Martin and Robert were stewards at this church.

Isom and Hudsonville were assigned the same pastor, Rev. Jackson. Sometime, if he could not get to Isom, for one reason or the other, the Stewart Board would call on a local preacher, Rev. Miles. Rev. Miles was a member of Isom Chapel and lived down several miles from the church on Isom Chapel Road.

YOU SOUND LIKE A PREACHER

You start with the Old
And end with the New
You open and close service with a hymn or two
Restating your text as the spirit moves you
You sure were called to preach
And you speak properly
You sound like a preacher to me

You talk of trials and tribulations
With the patience of Job
Relating events to the salvation of souls
You talk to the young about those pearly gates of gold
Asking for an Amen from the deacons-now and then
You wave to the sisters as they shout and wave their hands
You sound and look like a preacher to me

Your voice gets high and low
When bringing home a point
You pray in a whisper
Sometimes long-sometimes short
You strut back and Forth-Humming for awhile

When the congregation shouts, you end your text
Sounding just like a preacher

Rev. Miles was a "called" preacher, which meant he did not attend a school of theology. But, he still was dynamic and well known preacher. Rev. Miles and his wife, Mamie, had 12 children. They were a well-known singing family that formed a group called The Miles Singers. Within this group, their sons formed The Miles Quartet which would be invited to sing in churches as far away as Memphis. They always hosted family reunions at their home which drew large crowds other than family from the community and beyond. Singing by their family would be the main draw. They would plan this reunion on odd years Fourth of July weekend. This was done to avoid conflict with the one hosted by Hannah and Ralph, since the same people usually attended both reunions.

     GLORIA GIPSON SUGGS

Kimbrough Chapel Missionary Baptist Church

Kimbrough CME Baptist Church was located west on Kimbrough Chapel Road, just southwest of Atway Store. It was a sister church to Gatewood Chapel and sometimes they shared the same pastors and musicians. Kimbrough Chapel held service on the Fourth Sunday in each month and the revival the fourth week in August. Russell was head deacon and Vera sat on the motherboard. They were friends of Peter's parents, Jacob and Sara from Gatewood Chapel. Revival services were held Monday through Friday nights at all the churches during the week of revival. Kimbrough Chapel was no exception.

Come on mourners and join the army
The sermons are fiery and the hymns have harmony
We'll pray and sing all night if there is hope for you
Come on, mourner-join the army

You have been on the mourner's bench
Every day since Monday
Two preachers have preached
One came down with hoarseness
It's Friday night
Baptizing is Sunday
There were seven at the start of revival
Six have confessed
You are the only one left
Now is the time for you to join the rest

Come on mourner and join the army
It's Just about midnight and time for the benediction
We'll sing one more song and pray one more prayer
Please, come on, mourner, we're tired, sleepy, and hungry

Gatewood and Kimbrough Churches would co-host the local Baptist Conventions. It would be held over a period of several days leading up to the 4th Sunday service. Sarah and Vera would make plans with the motherboard members of other churches to insure enough food, table clothes, and chinaware would be prepared and brought for "dinner on the ground" after Sunday service. Jacob and Russell would make plans with the deacon board to be sure that enough tables and chairs were available for set up immediately after service.

Children's Day Programs were big to at Kimbrough Church. The children from Kimbrough and surrounding churches were always invited and encouraged to attend and participate. This church, like the other churches in the area, knew that children were the community's future leaders. So, most of the activities in these churches always involved children.

Every once in a while, shy children would come up with reasons not to give speeches. But, they wanted to participate in some way in the program.

I Can Ring Those Church Bells

I can't sing the song you gave me
I can't pick peaches from the trees
Finding my way around this place
Sometimes can be a task for me
I sure can't get honey from bees
But I can ring those church bells

I am too short to erase the blackboard
I am too small to lace my own shoes
Making clothes is out of the question
I am too young to vote
That bag is too big for me to tote
But I can ring those church bells

I can't make Children's Day speeches
I am afraid to lead that song
I can say The Lord's Prayer
But not out loud
I am downright afraid of crowds
I can ring those church bells

The end of revival at Kimbrough Chapel would signal the beginning of the harvest in September. Everybody in the community would focus on preparing for the winter to come. Peter, Rhea, and the other community members, would talk about the good times they experienced at the 4 churches during revival time. These revivals helped to prepare them spiritually for the days and years ahead.